The Boy, the mole, the Fox and the Horse

The Animated Story

This book is dedicated
to you, the reader.
Always remember you matter,
and you bring to this world
things no one else can.

THE BOY, THE MOLE, THE FOX AND THE HORSE
THE ANIMATED STORY

Charlie Mackesy

Hello

I hope you're ok, wherever you are in the world. A while ago I wrote a book – which was a surprise as I'm not good at reading them.

It's about a boy, a mole, a fox and a horse. The boy is lonely, lost and full of questions, when he first meets the mole. The mole is in love with cake. The fox is silent and wary because he's been hurt by life. The horse is the most powerful thing they have ever seen, but also the kindest.

They spend time together on an adventure in the wild. The truth is, I wasn't sure how the book would be received, but the surprise and wonder of it all was that some people liked it.

So we decided to make a film inspired by the book. The journey of animating the characters and bringing them to life has been an adventure I never imagined I'd have. The wonderfully gifted people I worked with were kind as I was completely out of my depth. ...

But in the end we did it. 🍰🍶
And so here we are. This is the book
of the film we made. I hope you
enjoy it and it encourages you somehow
– maybe even lifts you or reminds you
of the film if you've seen it. And if
you haven't seen it, I hope you like
the book anyway.

Thank you and much love to you.

Charlie x

"Hello."

"Hello", said the boy.

"What are you doing here?"
asked the mole.

"I'm lost," said the boy.

"Oh dear, well, that's no good."

"So... how did you get here?"
asked the mole.

"Well ... hello."

"Hello who?"

"Hello Cake".

"What cake?"
asked the boy.

"That cake!
It looks delicious, spectacular!
I mean it's ... it's magnificent!"

"I can't see a cake,"
said the boy.

"It's...it's..."

"Oh...
It's a tree."

"It is a lovely tree and it
did look a bit like a cake."

"So yes, well, no cake,
and you're lost."

"Yes."

"An old mole once told me,
when you're lost, follow the river
and it will take you home."

"And if you happen
to see a cake while
you're up there..."

"I'm so sorry," said the boy.

"Ahchoo! Oh no, I'm sorry," replied the mole.

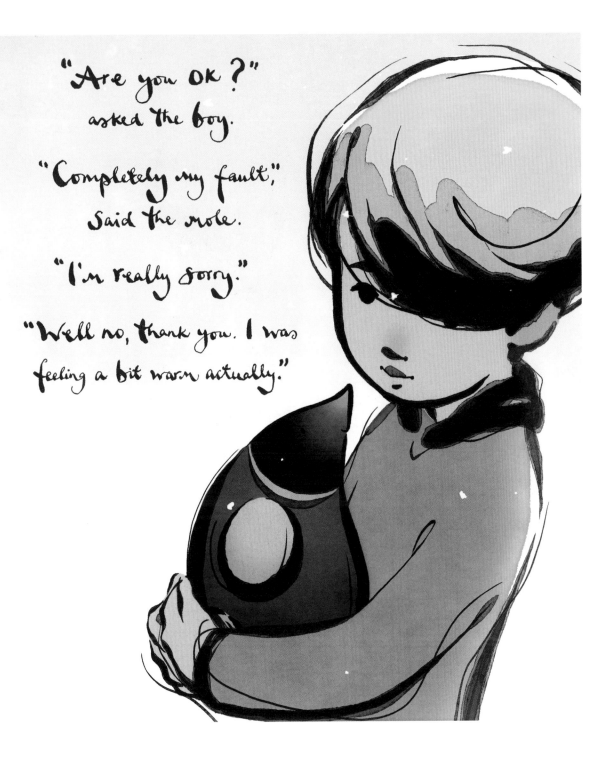

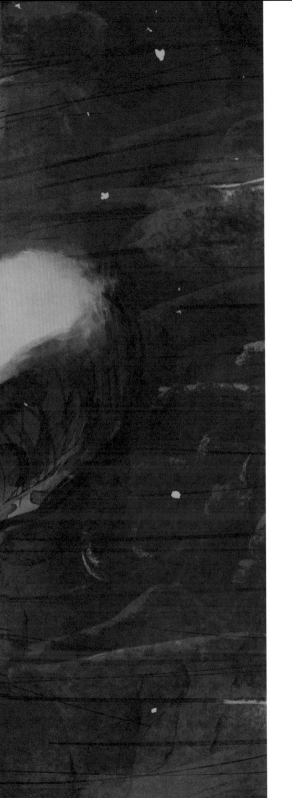

"What can you see?"
said the mole.

"Nothing really."

"Oh."

"Kind", said the boy.

"Mmm," said the mole.

"Nothing beats kindness.
It sits quietly beyond all things."

"So much beauty we need to look after," said the mole.

"Yes, so much."

"Ooof!"

"Are you alright?"

"Sorry, yes totally fine -
just thought we should start
looking for that river."

"Lemon drizzle,
this is quite a hill."

"Is this better?"
asked the boy.

"Well, I don't want to
be too much trouble."

"It's OK."

"Well, thank you."

"What is that over there?"

"It's the wild," said the mole.
"Don't fear it."

"Look, I can see a river!"
said the boy.

"Wait...what?
... I said don't fear it,
not charge straight at it!
I mean really. Good grief."

"Do you have a favourite saying?"
asked the boy.

"Yes," said the mole.

"What is it?"

"If at first you don't succeed,
have some cake."

"I see. Does it work?"

"Every time."

"Did the old mole say which way
we should follow?" asked the boy.

"I didn't ask her that."

"Oh."

"Isn't it odd, we can only see our outsides but nearly everything happens on the inside."

"Is there something there?"
asked the boy.
"It's getting dark."

"Shall we, um....?"

"Good idea."

"We can set off
properly tomorrow,"
said the mole.

"Imagine how we would be if we were less afraid," said the boy.

"Most of the old moles I know wish they'd listened less to their fears and more to their dreams," replied the mole. "What do you dream about?"

"Home," said the boy.

"Oh, what's that like?"

"I don't know. I'm not sure."

"mmm."

"But I know I need one."

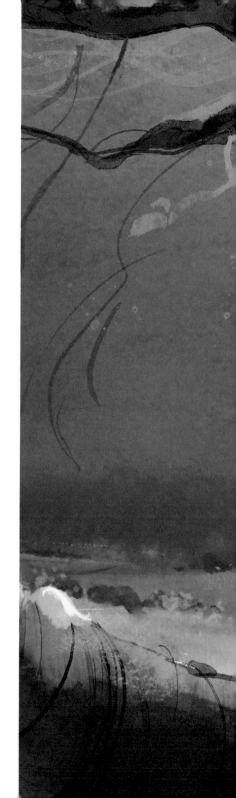

"Oh golly."

"He looks hungry,"
said the mole.

"He does."

"It's OK.
The fox has gone,"
said the boy.

"What was that sound??" asked the boy.
"I'm not sure."

"Do you think someone is hurt?"
"Maybe."
"Should we go and check?"

"Good idea. I'll stay in here to keep you warm."

"OK," said the boy. "Thank you."

"It's the fox,"
said the boy.
"He's trapped."

"Oh dear," whispered the mole.
"Please be careful," said the boy.
"I'm not afraid, I'm not afraid,
I am not afraid," said the mole.

"If I wasn't caught in this snare
I'd kill you," said the fox.

"If you stay in that snare
you'll ... die," said the mole.

So the Mole chewed through
the wire with his tiny teeth.

" You did so well."

"One of our greatest freedoms
is how we react to things,"
said the mole.

"Oooh, lovely morning!"
said the mole.

"Shall we get going?"

"Whoops! you're rolling"
cried the boy. "You look like
a snowball, no a Moleball.
A snow mole ... Stop rolling!"

"Goodness me!"
Said the mole.

"Oh gosh no, the river.
look out!"

"Thank you,"
said the mole.

"Thank you,"
said the boy.

"Oh, the fox is back.
Do you think he's coming
with us?" asked the boy.

"Oh, I do hope so."

"Maybe he's lost too."

"Well I think everyone
feels a bit lost sometimes,"
said the mole. "I know I do."

"I know what a
home looks like,"
said the mole.

"Do you?"

"Yes, it has walls, a roof,
a bell above the door, and
cakes in every window."

"I think that's a cake
shop," said the boy.

"Oh, is that not a type of home?"

"You can't live in a cake shop."

"Well, why ever not?"

"I think home is somewhere warm
and kind, with lights."

"Oh," said the mole.

"Hello."

"Hello."

"Have you been here a
while?" asked the boy.

"It feels that way,"
said the horse.

"Are you lost?"

"No."

"We are," said the mole,
"but we... have a plan."

"Ooooh, the snow on the trees –
it really does look just like icing,"
said the mole.

"You're obsessed!"

"Doing nothing with friends
is never doing nothing, is it?"
said the boy.

"No," replied the mole.

"I am so small," said the mole.

"Yes," replied the boy,
"but you make a huge difference."

"So, what are we doing?"
asked the horse.

"We are on a quest for cake,"
replied the mole.

"Are you now?"

"No, not really. We're following
the river to find a home."

"How far is it?"

"We... don't know," said the boy.

"Well, let's get going then."

"How fast can you run?" asked the boy.

"Well," said the mole, "I wouldn't say I was a natural athlete but I did once win a digging competition."

"I don't mean you!"
"Oh I see," said the mole.

"Oh golly,"
said the mole.

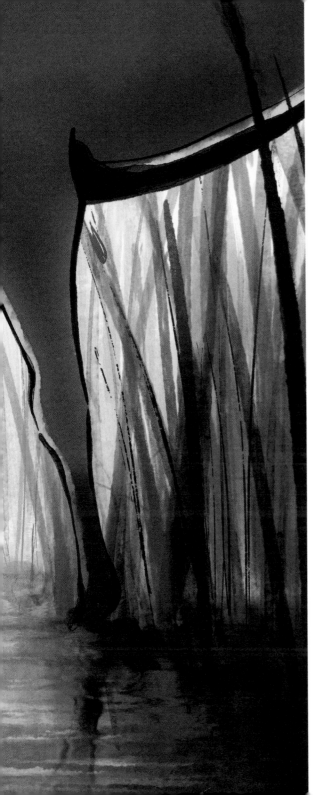

"You fell...
but I've got you."

"Sorry," said the boy.

"It was an accident,"
said the mole.

"It's my fault. I let go,"
said the boy.
"Oh gosh. Sorry. Sorry."

"Ah now," said the horse.

"Tears fall for a reason
and they are your strength
not weakness."

"I think you believe in me more than I do," said the boy.

"You'll catch up."

"Life is difficult,
but you are loved."

"Look! lights!
That looks like a home."

"Yes it does, doesn't it?"
said the mole.

"The fox never really speaks,"
whispered the boy.

"No. And it's lovely he is with us,"
said the horse.

"To be honest, I often feel
I have nothing interesting
to say," said the fox.

"Being honest is always interesting,"
said the horse.

"What's the bravest thing
you've ever said?"
asked the boy.

"Help," said the horse.

"Asking for help isn't giving up,"
said the horse,
"It's refusing to give up."

"Sometimes I want to say...
I love you all," said the mole,
"but I find it difficult."

"Do you?" said the boy.

"Yes, so I say something like,
I'm glad we are all here."

"OK," said the boy.

"I'm glad we are all here,"
said the mole.

"We are so glad you are here too."

"What should we do?"
asked the boy.
"That didn't sound good."

"When the big things feel out of control...

...focus on what you love right under
your nose," said the horse.

"This storm will pass."

"Oh no, where are the lights?
I can't see them anymore."

"It feels like we have such
a long way to go."

"I know," said the horse,
"but look how far we've come."

"I just don't think I can do this,"
said the boy, "I am never going to
find a home."

"You know," said the fox, "Sometimes your mind plays tricks on you. It can tell you you're no good, that it's hopeless..."

"... But I've discovered this - you are loved and important and you bring to this world things no one else can. So hold on."

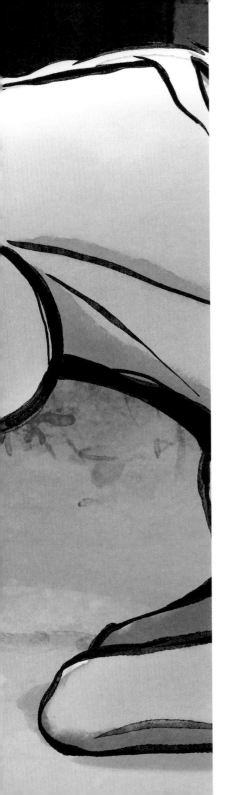

"Are you alright?"
asked the boy.

"There is something
I haven't told you,"
said the horse.

"What?"

"I can fly."

"You can fly?"

"Yes, but I stopped because it
made the other horses jealous."

"Well, we love you whether
you can fly or not."

"Come and join us,"
said the boy.

"Oh, I think I'll stay here,"
said the fox. "Thank you."

"Please?"

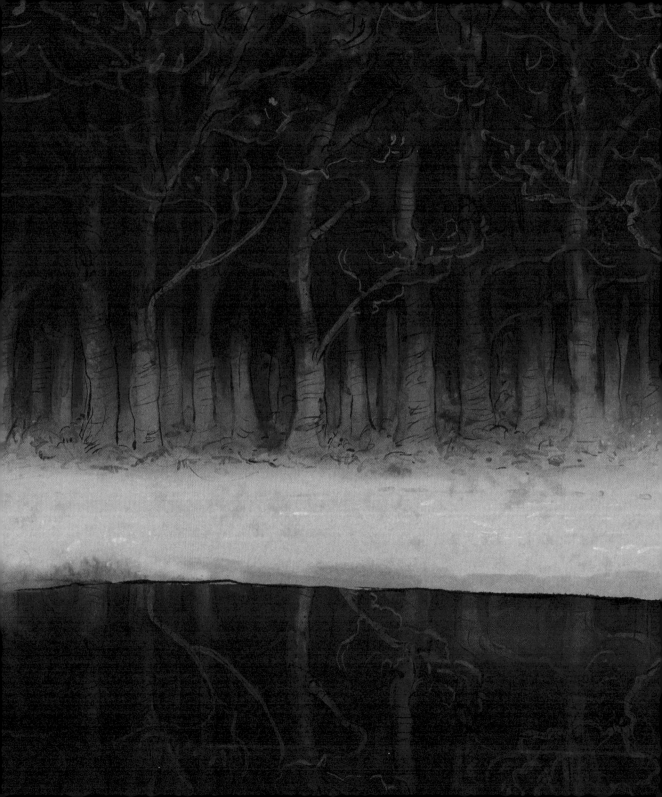

"Look. There it is!"
said the horse.

"You've found it!"
said the boy.

"It looks like a home,
doesn't it?" said the boy.

"Well", said the mole,
"here we are then."

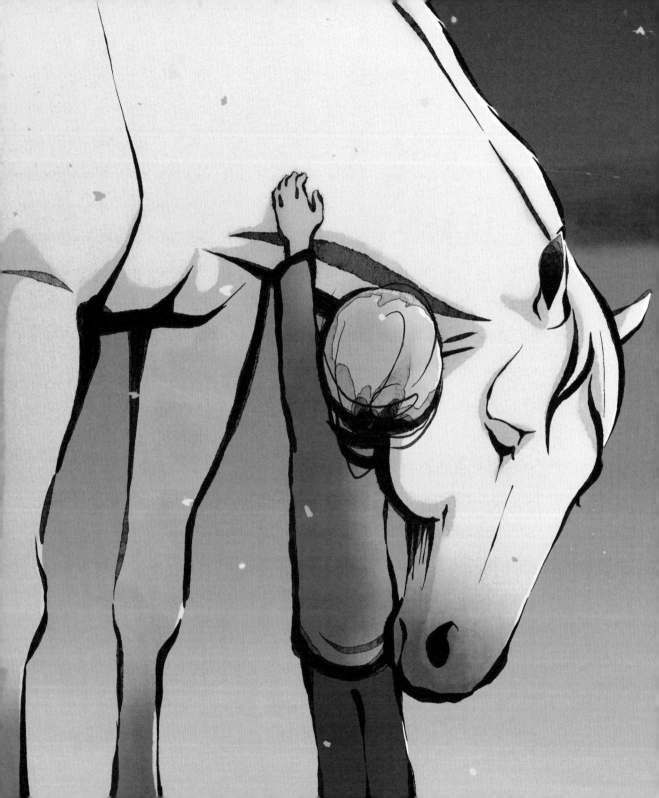

"Thank you", said the boy.

"Goodbye."

"Always remember, you're enough just as you are," said the fox.

"I'm glad we're all here,"
said the mole.

"I'm so glad you're here too."

"Goodbye," said the boy.
"I'm really going to miss you."

"Home isn't always
a place, is it?"

"Well, this is warm,"
said the mole.

"And very kind,"
replied the fox.

"And look at the stars,"
said the horse.

"So you know all about
me?" asked the boy.

"Yes," replied the horse.

"And you still love me?"

"We love you all the more."

"That's why we are here, isn't it?"
said the boy.

"For cake?" asked the mole.

"To love... and be loved."

THE BOY, THE MOLE, THE FOX AND THE HORSE

A Matthew Freud Production | *A Charlie Mackesy Film*

Directed by
PETER BAYNTON &
CHARLIE MACKESY

Produced by
CARA SPELLER
MATTHEW FREUD
J.J. ABRAMS & HANNAH MINGHELLA

Adapted by
JON CROKER & CHARLIE MACKESY

Art Director
MIKE McCAIN

Background Artists
JULIEN DE MAN
YINFAOWEI HARRISON
SUZIE KELLETT
LIA MCHEDLISHVILI
ALEXANDRIA NEONAKIS
ŁUKASZ PAZERA
ROMY YAO
JENNY YU

Visual Development
PETER BAYNTON
MIKE McCAIN
ANDREA MINELLA
TIM WATTS

Story Artists
PETER BAYNTON
ANDREW BROOKS
KARTIKA MEDIANI
WILLIAM SALAZAR
ROB STEVENHAGEN
ARJAN WILSCHUT

Layout Artists
MARCO CASTIELLO
NORBERT MAIER
SERGIO MANCINELLI
LIA MCHEDLISHVILI
NEAL PETTY
HANNES STUMMVOLL

Animation Supervisors
TIM WATTS
GABRIELE ZUCCHELLI

Animators
MARLÈNE BEAUBE
JEREMIE BECQUER
MURRAY DEBUS
TIM DILLNUTT
GARY DUNN
BISHOY GENDI
DARYL GRAHAM
REG ISAAC
LAURENT KIRCHER
PETER LOWEY

Animators – continued
ANDY McCOLL MCPHERSON
FERNANDO MORO
WILLIAM SALAZAR
MARIO SERRANO HERVAS
ANDREA SIMONTI
MARIA TORREGROSA DOMENECH
THIERRY TORRES RUBIO
TIM WATTS
ANDREAS WESSEL-THERHORN
PAUL WILLIAMS
GABRIELE ZUCCHELLI

FX Animator
RAYMOND PANG

Clean Animation Supervisor
SETAREH ERFAN

Lead Key Ink Animator
ANDREA MINELLA

Clean Animation Leads
DAVID LEICK-BURNS
JAY WREN

Key Ink Animators
JUDIT BOOR
KATERINA KREMASIOTI
JESSICA LESLAU
ALISON OXBORROW
PATRICK SELBY

Clean Animation Artists
CHRISTOPHER ABOIRALOR
MAGUI ALONSO
ALEXANDRA SASHA BALAN
NILI BHAVSAR
BEATRICE BORGHINI
VICTORIA BUDGETT
RON CHEVARIE
HARRY DAVIDSON
ANGELINE DE SILVA
LOIS DE SILVA
NICOLA JANE FRANCIS
ANDREA FRIEDRICH
GERRY GALLEGO
PAFO GALLIERI
RAQUEL JUAN MAESTRE
LAUREN KIRKWOOD
SAFFRON MACKIE
LISA O'SULLIVAN
NATASHA POLLACK
GEMMA ROBERTS
ESTEFANÍA ROMÓN
CLARA SCHILDHAUER
KATHERINE SPANGENBERG
CRISTINA URSACHI
ASH J. WU

Clean Animation Artist – Tones
KATARZYNA MENCFEL-WENGLARCZYK

Clean Animation Artists – Mattes
LEROY AYTON
LEWIS CAMPBELL
JACK LANGRIDGE GOULD
WAYNE MASLIN
MONICA SCANLAN
FABIOLA TENORIO

Clean Animation Artists – Shadows
JENNIFER DUCZMAL
ANDREW STADLER
DAVID WEGMANN-SERIN

Lead Compositor
NICK HERBERT

Compositors
MARTIAL COULON
VALÉRIE GUICHARD
NAYRA PARDO ONATE
JOHNNY STILL

Line Producers
DIMITRI ANASTASAKIS
ELLEN COLLINS

Production Managers
DELPHI LYTHGOE
JULIE MURNAGHAN

Production Coordinator
ANNA FITZSIMONS

Additional Production Support
LIZ MACKE

Production Accountant
IWONA SOBIECKA

Development Coordinator
DELPHI LYTHGOE

VFX Supervisor
NEIL RILEY

Specialist Systems Support
BENEDICT WOOD

Editor
DANIEL BUDIN

Music Composed by
ISOBEL WALLER-BRIDGE

*Sound Designer, Sound Mixer
& Sound Editor*
ADRIAN RHODES

Colourist
THOMAS URBYE

Acknowledgements

There are so many incredible people who contributed
to this book, it's hard to know where to begin.
Thank you - Matthew, Callan, Helen, Rhydian and Louise.
To the brilliant Colin, who sewed the book together. ♡
Thank you to the whole film team who
began as colleagues and ended as friends;
Cara, Peter, Delphi, Mike, Seti, Tim and Gabriele,
Nick, Andrea, Julie, Dimitri, Daniel, Jon,
Iso and Richard, Laura, Joel, Alice, Lucy, Becky and Lara.
Also JJ, Hannah and Jon. Thank you. 🎂 ♡
To everyone on social media for your enthusiasm.
And to Sara, Christopher and Daisy, and Barney,
Gracie and my lovely mum. ♡
Lastly, my thanks to you, the reader.
x

I

EBURY PRESS IS AN IMPRINT OF EBURY PUBLISHING,
20 VAUXHALL BRIDGE ROAD, LONDON SW1V 2SA

EBURY PRESS IS PART OF THE PENGUIN RANDOM HOUSE
GROUP OF COMPANIES WHOSE ADDRESSES CAN BE
FOUND AT GLOBAL.PENGUINRANDOMHOUSE.COM

FIRST PUBLISHED BY EBURY PRESS IN 2022

WWW.PENGUIN.CO.UK

A CIP CATALOGUE RECORD FOR THIS BOOK
IS AVAILABLE FROM THE BRITISH LIBRARY

ISBN 978 1 52919 768 6

DESIGN BY COLM ROCHE AT IMAGIST
COLOUR ORIGINATION BY ALTAIMAGE, LONDON
PRINTED AND BOUND IN ITALY BY L.E.G.O. S.P.A

THE AUTHORISED REPRESENTATIVE IN THE EEA IS
PENGUIN RANDOM HOUSE IRELAND, MORRISON CHAMBERS,
32 NASSAU STREET, DUBLIN D02 YH68

PENGUIN RANDOM HOUSE IS COMMITTED TO A
SUSTAINABLE FUTURE FOR OUR BUSINESS, OUR READERS
AND OUR PLANET. THIS BOOK IS MADE FROM FOREST
STEWARDSHIP COUNCIL® CERTIFIED PAPER.